INVESTIGATING
ELECTRICITY

SUPER COOL SCIENCE EXPERIMENTS

CHERRY LAKE PRESS
Ann Arbor, Michigan

by Sophie Lockwood

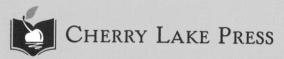

CHERRY LAKE PRESS

Published in the United States of America by
Cherry Lake Publishing Group
Ann Arbor, Michigan
www.cherrylakepublishing.com

Reading Adviser: Beth Walker Gambro, MS, Ed., Reading Consultant, Yorkville, IL

Content Editor: Robert Wolffe, EdD,
Professor of Teacher Education, Bradley University, Peoria, Illinois

Book Designer: Ed Morgan of Bowerbird Books

Grateful acknowledgment to Deborah Simon, Department of Chemistry, Whitman College

Photo Credits: cover and title page, 5, 6, 7, 12, 16, 20, 22, 23 24, 27, 28, 29, freepik. com; 4, 9, 10, 13, 14, 15, 17, 18, 19, 21, 25, 26, The Design Lab; 8, Lwilcoxson/ Wikimedia Commons; 11, Wikimedia Commons.

Cherry Lake Press is an imprint of Cherry Lake Publishing Group.

Library of Congress Cataloging-in-Publication Data has been filed and is available at catalog.loc.gov

Printed in the United States of America
Corporate Graphics

A Note to Parents and Teachers: Please review the instructions for these experiments before your children do them. Be sure to help them with any experiments you do not think they can safely conduct on their own.

A Note to Kids: Be sure to ask an adult for help with these experiments when you need it. Always put your safety first!

Note from Publisher: Websites change regularly, and their future contents are outside of our control. Supervise children when conducting any recommended online searches for extended learning opportunities.

CONTENTS

Lightning Bolts
AND VOLTS!

When humans first saw lightning bolts slice through the sky, they were probably shocked. Today, we know why lightning is so shocking. A bolt of lightning delivers up to 300 million **volts** of electric power! A typical American home only uses about 120 volts.

The great thinker and inventor Ben Franklin investigated electricity. He experimented with a kite, metal wire, and a key during a thunderstorm. Franklin's experiment helped us understand the connection between lightning and electricity better.

So what is electricity? It's a form of energy that comes from tiny particles called **electrons**. When electrons move, they create electricity. And electricity powers just about everything around you, including lights, cars, and computers.

Benjamin Franklin was born in 1706. He was a great thinker and inventor. He was also one of the founders of the United States.

Getting STARTED

We can learn more about electricity through experiments. If you want to find out how or why something works, you investigate it. Then you make **observations** and find a way to test your ideas. That is exactly what scientists do. In this book, we'll learn how to safely experiment with electricity. Let's get started!

When scientists design experiments, they often use the scientific method. What is the scientific method? It's a step-by-step process to answer specific questions. The steps don't always follow the same pattern. However, the scientific method often works like this:

STEP ONE: A scientist gathers the facts and makes observations about one particular thing.

STEP TWO: The scientist comes up with a question that is not answered by observations and facts.

STEP THREE: The scientist creates a **hypothesis**. This is a statement about what the scientist thinks might be the answer to the question.

STEP FOUR: The scientist tests the hypothesis by designing an experiment to see whether the hypothesis is correct. Then the scientist carries out the experiment and writes down what happens.

STEP FIVE: The scientist draws a **conclusion** based on the result of the experiment. The conclusion might be that the hypothesis is correct. Sometimes, though, the hypothesis is not correct. In that case, the scientist might develop a new hypothesis and another experiment.

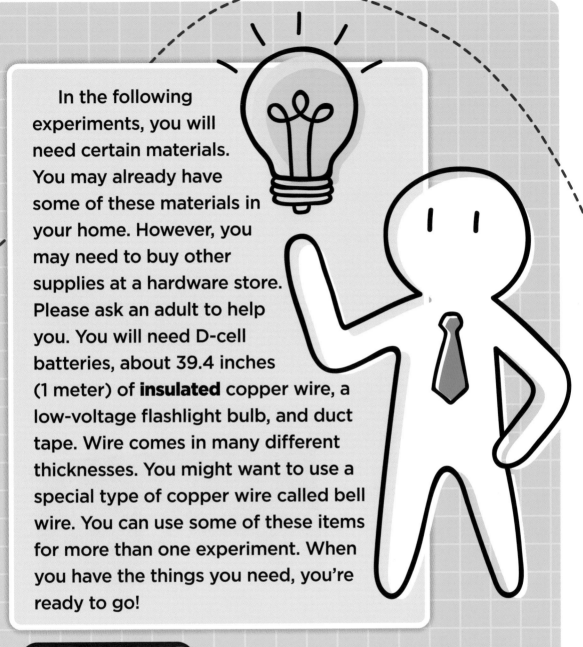

In the following experiments, you will need certain materials. You may already have some of these materials in your home. However, you may need to buy other supplies at a hardware store. Please ask an adult to help you. You will need D-cell batteries, about 39.4 inches (1 meter) of **insulated** copper wire, a low-voltage flashlight bulb, and duct tape. Wire comes in many different thicknesses. You might want to use a special type of copper wire called bell wire. You can use some of these items for more than one experiment. When you have the things you need, you're ready to go!

BE SAFE!

When you work with electricity, you must be very careful. Never perform experiments using electrical sockets in your house or a car battery. Instead, use household batteries. D-cell batteries are safer to handle. Also, ask an adult to help you!

EXPERIMENT 1

Shocking!

Have you ever gotten a shock walking across a carpet or getting out of a car? If so, you have experienced static electricity. All electricity is the flow of electrons in matter. Static electricity shock comes from the release or discharge of electrons.

Static electricity is electricity that is made by rubbing two substances together. Let's create an experiment to test static electricity. Will rubbing any two substances together make static electricity? Our hypothesis is: **Only certain substances will create static electricity.**

Static electricity can make a person's hair stand on end!

Here's what you'll need:

- A balloon
- A cup of popped rice cereal
- A piece of plain paper
- A handful of packing peanuts
- A silk scarf
- A wooden spoon
- A piece of 100-percent wool material

· INSTRUCTIONS ·

1. Blow up the balloon and tie it. Rub the balloon very quickly against the top of your head. Gently pull the balloon away from your head. What happens to your hair?

2. Sprinkle some puffed rice cereal on a piece of paper. Sprinkle a handful of packing peanuts on a table.

3. Quickly rub the surface of the balloon with the wool. Pass the balloon about 1 inch (2.5 centimeters) above the cereal. What happens? Place the balloon about 1 inch (2.5 cm) above the packing peanuts. What happens?

4. Quickly rub the balloon with the silk scarf. Pass the balloon about 1 inch (2.5 cm) above the puffed rice cereal. What happens? Place the balloon about 1 inch above the packing peanuts.

5. Put the balloon aside. Rub the wooden spoon against your hair and see what happens.

6. Quickly rub the surface of the wooden spoon with the wool. Pass the spoon over the cereal. Place the spoon over the packing peanuts. What do you observe?

· CONCLUSION ·

What observations did you make? Did you get the same results with the balloon and the wooden spoon? Think about the results of your experiment. Did the experiment prove or disprove the hypothesis?

Thomas Edison was a famous inventor and businessman who worked with electricity.

FACTS!

Sometimes, an experiment does not work. The result can be unexpected. Someone once said to Thomas Edison that many of his experiments were failures. Edison replied, "I have not failed. I have just found 10,000 ways that won't work."

· EXPERIMENT 2 ·

Checking the Charge

Everything in the universe is made up of atoms. Inside the atoms are particles called protons, electrons, and neutrons. Protons carry a positive electrical charge. Electrons carry a negative electrical charge. Neutrons carry no charge. The ends of magnets also have positive and negative charges. When you work with magnets, two like ends push away from each other. Opposite ends attract each other.

If two objects carry the same charge, how will they react when they are close to each other? To test for the effects, we'll need to make an electroscope. That is an instrument used by scientists to measure an electric charge. You are going to test the effect of a charge on the electroscope. Here is one possible hypothesis: **The charges will work like magnets. Like charges will force aluminum strips away from each other.**

Here's what you'll need:

- Scissors
- A clear, deep plastic container with a flexible plastic lid
- Aluminum foil
- A large metal paper clip
- Modeling clay or duct tape
- A balloon
- A piece of 100-percent wool fabric

· INSTRUCTIONS ·

1. Use the scissors to make a small hole in the center of the plastic lid. The hole should be large enough for the paper clip to pass through.

2. Cut two strips of aluminum foil that measure roughly 0.5 (1.3 cm) by 2 inches (5 cm). Unfold the paper clip so that it looks like a long J. Use the straight end of the paper clip to punch a small hole in one end of each foil strip. Hang the foil strips on the curved end of the paper clip.

3. Insert the straight part of the J paper clip through the hole in the plastic lid. When you put the lid on the container, the foil strips should hang freely inside the container. Use modeling clay or duct tape to firmly secure the paper clip to the lid. When you are done, the foil strips should hang in the center of the container without touching the sides or bottom.

4. Crumple a 4-inch (10 cm) square piece of aluminum foil onto the end of the paper clip that sticks out from the container. Your electroscope is ready.

14

5. Blow up the balloon. Give the balloon a charge by rubbing it with a piece of wool. Slowly bring the charged balloon near the foil ball on the electroscope. What happens to the foil strips inside the container? Write down the results of the experiment.

CONCLUSION

Did the foil strips move when the charged balloon came near the foil ball? How did they move? Was our hypothesis right? Can you think of some other experiments you could perform using the electroscope? Could you measure the strength of an electrical charge? What would you look for?

· EXPERIMENT 3 ·

Battery Power

In Experiments #1 and #2, you learned how to generate static electricity. But you can't run a car or a TV using static electricity. For that, you need an electric **current**. When scientist Alessandro Volta experimented with electric current, he found a way to produce electricity. Volta's discovery was a battery! He used acid and metal to make his battery.

Do you think you can generate electricity from items you have in your own house? Citrus fruits, such as lemons and oranges, have acid in their juice. Let's build a battery using lemons, pennies, and paper clips. Do you think it will work? Here's a hypothesis: **It is possible to make a battery using the acid in lemons and metal objects found in homes.**

Here's what you'll need:

- 3 pieces of insulated copper wire, 12 inches (30 cm) long
- A small battery-powered digital clock (with no battery)
- A pair of scissors or wire strippers
- 2 large metal paper clips
- 2 clean pennies
- 2 large lemons
- 2 small pieces of duct tape
- A marker
- A butter knife

· INSTRUCTIONS ·

1. Ask an adult for help before you start. You will need to remove about 2 inches (5 cm) of insulation from each end of the 3 pieces of wire. Have an adult do this by *carefully* cutting the wire insulation with the wire strippers or scissors. Do *not* cut through the wire.

2. Wrap one end of Wire #1 around one paper clip. Wrap one end of Wire #2 around a penny. Using Wire #3, wrap one end around the second paper clip and the other end around the second penny.

3. Using pressure from your hands to make the fruit softer, roll each lemon against the counter.

4. With an adult, use the butter knife to cut two **parallel** slits (A and B) about 1 inch (2.5 cm) apart in each lemon. Cut the slits along the width of the lemons, not lengthwise.

5. Working from left to right, mark the lemons #1 and #2 with a marker. Mark the slits A and B on each lemon.

6. In Slit A of Lemon #1, insert the penny attached to Wire #2. Using Wire #3, with both a paper clip and a penny attached, insert the paper clip into Slit B of Lemon #1.

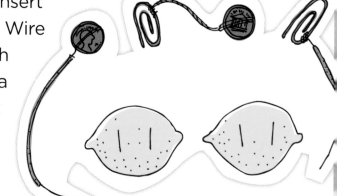

7. Insert the penny attached to Wire #3 into Slit A of Lemon #2. Using Wire #1, insert the paper clip into Slit B of Lemon #2. From left to right, you should have 2 lemons with 1 penny and 1 paper clip inserted in each.

8. Now, look at the clock. There will be small marks (+ and -) that indicate the positive (+) and the negative (-) **terminals** where the battery goes. Use duct tape to attach the end of Wire #2 (from the penny) to the negative terminal. Attach the end of Wire #1 to the positive terminal. Now everything should be connected. What happens now that the **circuit** is no longer open? Write down your results.

CONCLUSION

Did your lemon battery work? If it did, you proved our hypothesis. It is possible to make a battery using lemons and metal objects you have at home. Does your conclusion make you think of any new questions?

· EXPERIMENT 4 ·

Kitchen Conductors

Electricity is all around you. In fact, you **generate** electricity in your body every day! Your brain and nerves send electrical signals throughout your body to warn you about pain, cold, and heat, for example. Electricity is an amazing form of energy. Any substance that allows electricity to flow through it is a conductor. Your body is a conductor. So are other materials such as metal.

Let's design an experiment that tests conductors. What makes a good conductor? Here is one hypothesis: **Only metal makes a good conductor.** Here is another hypothesis: **Rubber is a poor conductor of electricity.**

Here is an experiment to test the first hypothesis.

Here's what you'll need:

- 3 pieces of insulated copper wire, about 12 inches (30 cm) each
- Various household items, such as a pickle, a potato, a rubber band, a wooden spoon, a metal spoon, and a new penny
- A pair of scissors or a wire strippers
- Duct tape
- A D-cell battery
- A flashlight bulb
- A butter knife

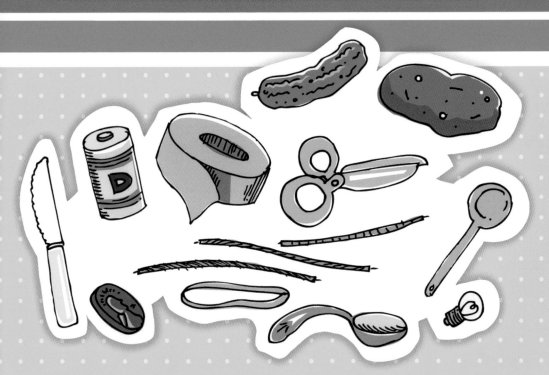

· INSTRUCTIONS ·

1. As you did in Experiment #3, ask an adult to help you strip the wire. *Carefully* cut the wire insulation about 2 inches (5 cm) from each end with scissors or wire strippers. Remember not to cut through the wire. Gently pull the insulation off the end of the wire.

2. Use duct tape to attach Wire #1 to one end of the battery. Attach Wire #2 to the other end of the battery with tape. Twist the free end of Wire #2 and one end of Wire #3 together. Wrap the twisted wire ends around the bottom of a flashlight bulb and tape them in place. Test your connections by completing, or closing, the circuit. Touch the free ends of Wires #1 and #3 together. Does the bulb light up? If not, check each wire to make sure it is secure.

3. When you get the flashlight bulb to light, you are ready to test your conductors. *Carefully* cut 2 small slits, about 1 inch (2.5 cm) apart, in the pickle. Insert the free ends of Wires #1 and #3 into the slits in the pickle. Write down your results. Repeat this process to test each of the other household items you have gathered. Make sure to write down the results for each item.

CONCLUSION

Review your results. Which items were good conductors of electricity? What was your conclusion?

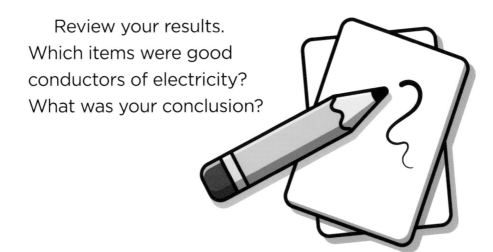

EXPERIMENT 5

Cool Circuits

Now that you know about batteries and conductors, let's see if we can wire some circuits. Circuits only work when they are connected in the right way. There are two types of circuits: series circuits and parallel circuits. A series circuit connects items along one path. A parallel circuit connects items in a side-by-side pattern.

Here's a hypothesis: **If one part of a series circuit is broken (the circuit is opened), the circuit doesn't work. If part of a parallel circuit is broken, other parts will still work.** Now, try to prove your hypothesis!

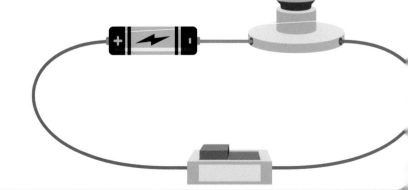

Here's what you'll need:

- 2 new pennies
- 7 strips of aluminum foil, 1 inch (2.5 cm) by 12 inches (30 cm)
- Duct tape
- 2 D-cell batteries
- 4 flashlight bulbs
- 3 large metal paper clips

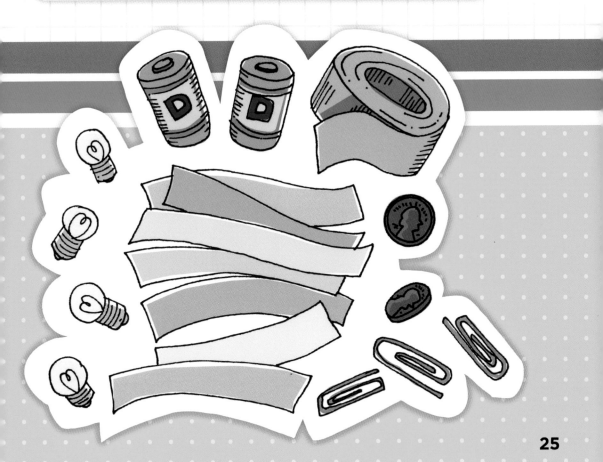

1. **Make a series circuit:** Wrap 1 penny at the end of Foil Strip #1. Tape the wrapped penny to the negative (–) end of a battery. Fold the free end of that foil strip over Foil Strip #2 and place a flashlight bulb on the fold. Tighten the foil around the end of the bulb and secure it with a piece of tape. Wrap the free end of Foil Strip #2 around the second bulb and secure it with tape. You now have the following connection: battery—foil—bulb—foil—bulb.

2. Now, attach Foil Strip #3 to the positive (+) end of the battery with tape. Wrap the free end of that strip around 1 paper clip. Make sure the connections are tight.

3. Touch the paper clip to the bottom of the second bulb. What happens? Write down your results.

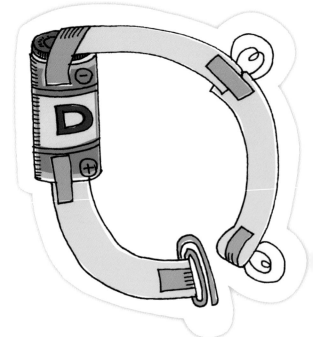

4. **Make a parallel circuit:** Wrap the other penny at the end of Foil Strip #4. Tape the wrapped penny to the negative (–) end of the second battery. Wrap one end of Foil Strip #5 around the bottom of the third flashlight bulb. Repeat that step with Foil Strip #6 and the fourth bulb. Using the second paper clip, attach the free end of Strip #5 to the middle of Strip #4. Attach the free end of Strip #6 to the end of Strip #4 with the third paper clip. Tape Foil Strip #7 to the positive (+) end of the battery.

5. Now you can test your circuit. Touch the foil-wrapped bottom of one bulb to Strip #7. What happens? Repeat this step with the other bulb. What happens? Touch both bulbs to Strip #7 at the same time. What did you learn?

CONCLUSION

Did you prove your hypothesis? When your series circuit was broken, did both bulbs light? Why or why not? What happened when you made a parallel circuit? What do you think explains your answer?

How does what you learned apply to your home? For example, if you turn on the kitchen light, will the toaster also turn on? Hopefully not! Your home should be wired with parallel circuits.

EXPERIMENT 6

Do It Yourself!

Now you know you can make your own battery. You can also make circuits! What other experiments can you safely do with the equipment you have? Would two batteries wired in a circuit make the flashlight bulbs glow brighter? Design an experiment to find out.

If your experiment doesn't work, don't worry. Like Thomas Edison, you have discovered something that doesn't work. Learn from it, and keep on experimenting, young scientist!

FACTS!

Electricity can be made from all types of things, including water, wind, and the Sun. The Sun makes enough energy in just 1 hour to power the whole world for a year! Scientists are still working on how to capture all that energy.

Glossary

circuit (SUR-kit) a path that carries an electric current from a source to the devices that are being run by electricity and then back to the source

conclusion (kuhn-KLOO-zhuhn) a final decision, thought, or opinion

current (KUR-rent) the flow of electricity that comes from an ordered, directional movement of electrical particles

electrons (ee-LEK-trahnz) subatomic particles with a negative electric charge

generate (JEN-ur-ayt) to produce

hypothesis (hy-POTH-uh-sihss) a logical guess about what will happen in an experiment

insulated (IN-suh-lay-ted) covered in a material that stops or reduces the movement of electricity

observations (ob-zur-VAY-shuhnz) things that are seen or noticed with one's senses

parallel (PA-ruh-lel) running side by side

terminals (TUR-mih-nuhlz) connection points on a battery

volts (VOHLTSS) units of electric power; the energy needed to drive one ampere of electric current against one unit of resistance

For More Information

BOOKS
Crane, Cody. *Electricity and Magnetism*. New York: Scholastic, 2019.

Dahl, Oyvind Nydal. *A Beginner's Guide to Circuits*. San Franciso, CA: No Starch Press, 2018.

Van Vleet, Carmella. *Electricity: Circuits, Static, and Electromagnets*. Norwich, VT: Nomad Press, 2022.

WEBSITES
Explore these online sources with an adult:

Britannica Kids: Electricity

NASA: 10 Interesting Things About Energy

PBS Kids: Electrical Circuit

Index

About the Author

Sophie Lockwood first experimented with electricity when she was in school. Her science teacher had the students build radios from scratch. She has been fascinated by electricity ever since. Today, she writes nonfiction books for children. Sophie thoroughly enjoyed testing these electrical experiments in her kitchen.